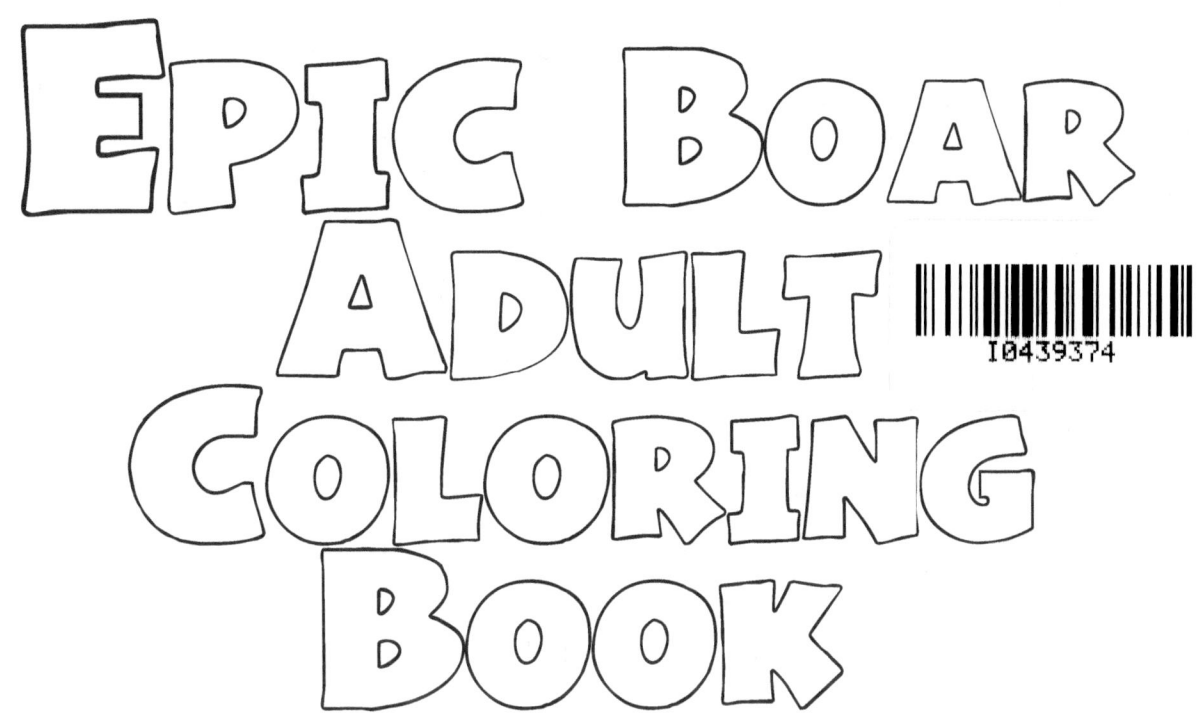

Epic Boar Adult Coloring Book

By Susan Potterfields

Copyright © 2016 Susan Potterfields

All rights reserved.

ISBN: 10: 1535091606
ISBN-13: 978-1535091602

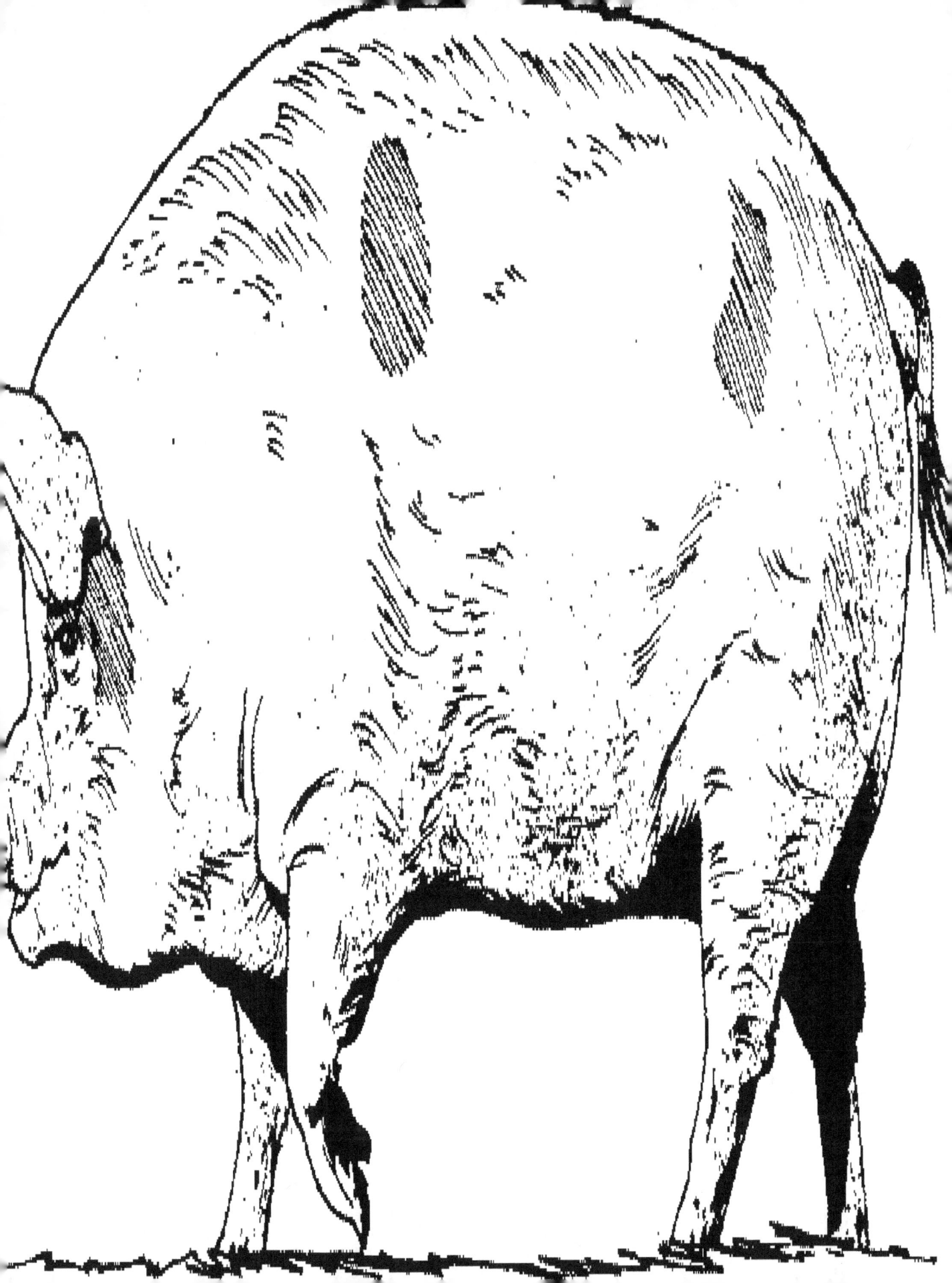

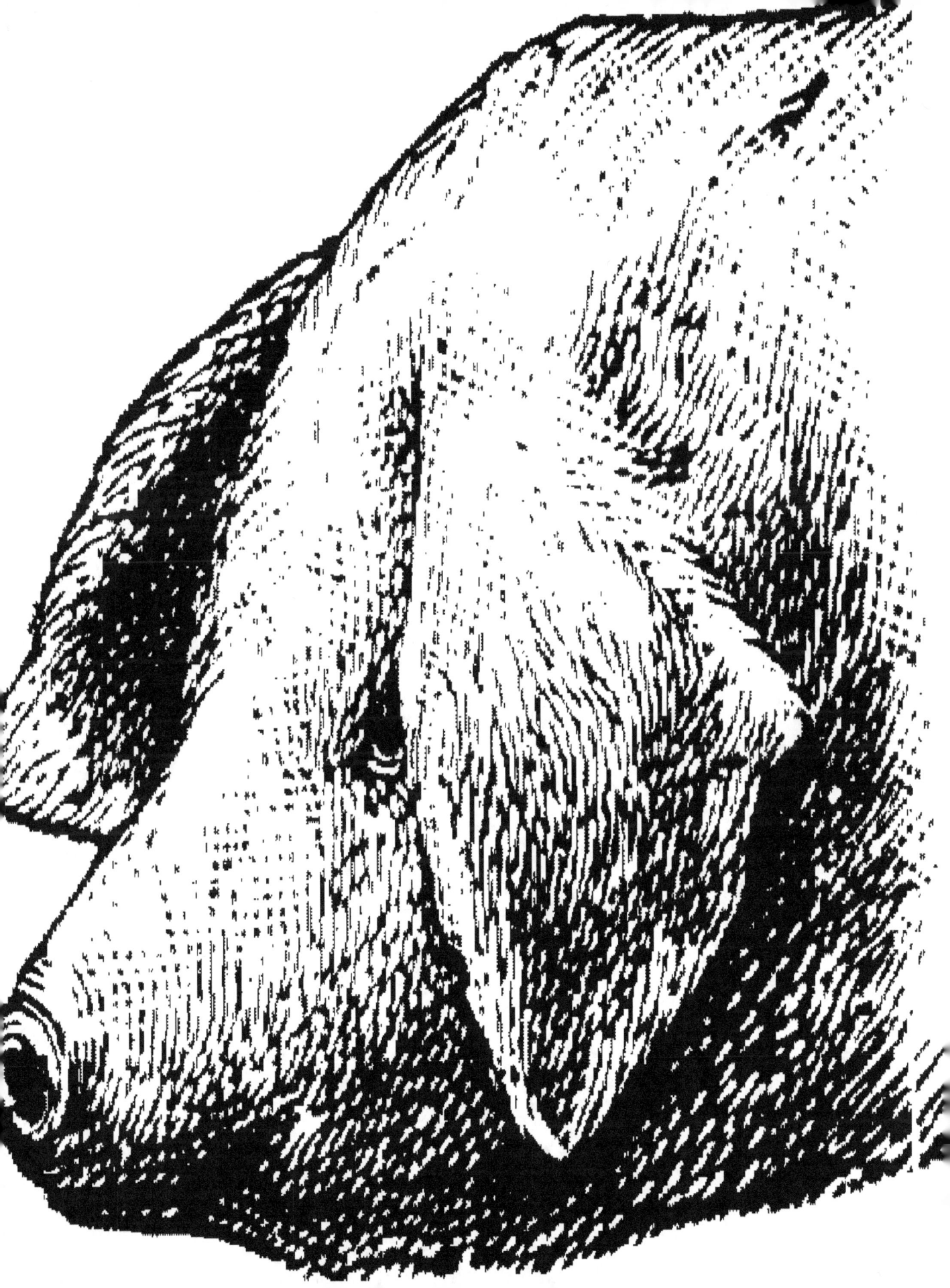

Other Coloring Books By Susan Potterfields

Epic Cat Adult Coloring Book
Epic Dog Adult Coloring Book
Epic Cow Adult Coloring Book
Epic Chicken Adult Coloring Book
Epic Dolphin Adult Coloring Book
Epic Crab Adult Coloring Book
Epic Bear Adult Coloring Book
Epic Turkey Adult Coloring Book

And Many More